Be Inspired;
A Closer Walk With God

by
Henry Sanders

I0111393

All poems contained in this book are registered with the Library of
Congress, Washington, DC

ISBN-13: 978-0-692-58929-8
ISBN-10: 0692589295

Published by
HOSWRITES
Florida
hoswrites.com

CONTENTS

CONTENTS

CONTENTS

ACKNOWLEDGMENT

I would like to thank God for His love, forgiveness, and for His many blessings none of which I deserve.

AUTHOR'S MESSAGE

This has truly been a labor of love. I hear that said often but I can now say that I know what it means to say it. I have been writing for many, many years but never have published anything; until now. I hope this book brings you a margin of inspiration and joy as you read through it but most of all, I hope you find it a little easier to move closer to God. After all, as Christians, isn't that our purpose?

Glory Days

When I look back on my life
I see many things
I see some smiles, some carefree days
and yes, there has been pain.
A humble start not much to show
but guidance with love and care
most needs met, on rainy days
and mom was always there.
I have not done marvelous things
not many know I'm alive.
I just sit here these remaining days
and look through tear filled eyes.
Friends and family, all but gone,
alone, left to endure.
I can hardly wait till the glory days
when I can begin my tour.
Oh, don't cry for me, don't shed a tear.
I've seen what this life has to show.
I get strength from the knowledge of
the angelic heavenly glow.
When it's time, I'll hurry on
I've waited too long for better things,
so I'll speed as fast as I possibly can
I'll fly with my wide spread wings.
I'll say good-bye to what I've known
and say hello to greater and more.
It's hard to be stuck with what I've got
when I know what I have in store.
I'll gladly give this up, for glory days,
eternity sounds so sweet;
after all, there's nothing that I want more
than to sit and wash his divine feet.

1

Faith

It's by grace for things unseen that we have faith.
Faith is hope, faith is trust;

to feel inside what you cannot explain
to accept with vigor what cannot be proven

to go by will to unknown places
to feel safe even in trepidation

the world at large is guided by faith
the hopes and dreams of a new generation

things that were, will be no more
the clouds will give way to sunshine

to those who don't own the armor of faith
these words are those of an optimist

let it be made crystal clear
faith is not optimism and vice versa

optimism is earthly
faith has its origin from higher

life is lived each day by faith
the hope that tomorrow will be brighter.

God, Please Don't Forget Me

I'm sorry GOD
I really truly am
for all the things I've done.

I have had
a good go of things
my life, my things, and fun.

I've promised things
that I've not done
and done things I am ashamed to have done.

And all through this
I've depended on
your promise through your Son.

I ask you now
to forgive again
and wipe my sin slate clean.

And give to me
a converted heart
and allow me to start again.

I try so hard
to make you proud
but self gets the best of me.

I still believe
that you're in control
so please don't give up on me.

I guess this is
a plea to you
to save a wretch like me.

And when you return
to gather your seed
please God, don't forget me.

Give Back to God

The mighty hands that shaped the void
and set the Sun to shine
that sprinkled the stars in the sky
belongs to our Father divine

all that is good starts with Him
the creator of the universes
the things He did and still will do
are covered throughout the verses

from healing, delivering, protecting us
the love He shows doesn't end
to guiding, teaching, forgiving us
truly a lover of men.

All He asks is to show the love
He faithfully shows us all
to care and respect for each as our own
and not to cause our brother to fall

to commit to Him like He has to us
to show His ways as our ways
to forgive those things done to us
and pray for an end to these days

He does not ask for more than we have
He gives us all we need
so give to Him what He gave us first
and enjoy our bountiful seed.

Henry Sanders

The Divine Plan

Have you given much serious thought,
to the destiny of your soul,
what happens after the life we live
and where do all of us go?

Can there be more to all of this,
or is it true that when you die, you're done?
And if that concept be true
why shouldn't we enjoy earthly fun?

Why give up the things you love,
the things that excite your carnal ways,
why walk the righteous narrow path
if there is nothing after the end of days?

Why love your fellow man
as you also love yourself
but really, where would we be
if that's how everyone felt?

I ask you to consider
with open mind and heart
that there was a divine plan
even from the very start.

Our Creator, GOD, who sits on high
gave to us a mortal life
and for the truly faithful ones
He promises eternal life.

One so different from the first
no pain or suffering, no sickness or death
no unkind acts or unkind thoughts
everyone restored to a perfect created health.

I know it's hard for your mind to conceive
something so far from what we know today
but I'm promised by the Mighty One,
that it really is that way.

Close your eyes, free your mind
let your senses go
imagine now a perfect place
and answers to whatever you don't know.

Nothing to want, that you won't have,
the ability to move about unrestrained
no sin, no destruction, no evil acts
no more heavy hearts filled with pain.

Anything perfect, good and righteous
all for your enjoyment
to talk and walk with GOD himself
the ultimate enjoyment.

If you've been inspired by what you felt
and you want to feel even more
then pray and read and search the book
and let the spirit reveal even more.

But if you feel no different than before
things still confusing to you
then repeat the process every day
and allow the spirit to speak to you.

Remembrance of the Cross

If the time has come,
for me to pay,
for the life that I
have lived

and to give an account
for the things I've done
and the people
I must forgive.

I pray that I
would have found,
the strength
to do as Jesus did.

To spread the word,
to spread some joy,
to live my life
as He did.

For in the end
when time does stop,
all efforts will
hence be lost,

so whilst I live,
here on earth,
I mustn't forget my purpose
I mustn't forget the cross.

In Spite of Adam and Eve

They stood in the mist of Paradise
no wants, no worries, no fear.
They had it all, as we recall,
the Maker always near.
An early morning walk
with inspirational talk
His direction was pretty clear…
of all else you may enjoy
but of this, this tree, right here,
I instruct you, not to eat.
For if you do, and I hope you won't
it will certainly deeply hurt me.
I will give to you all that you'll need
nothing of you to repay.
I created you and I love you
and I don't want it any other way.
But the she of he was lured away
and did the thing that started it all
and enticed the he of she

It's hard sometimes without seeing you,
this is what the disciples went through,
but I can wait, you've taught me how
but I want to see you now.

I rest in the assurance that your word gives,
that someday hence, if I die, I will live.
Oh what a glorious time that will be
when you come back for me.

I'll Have to Wait

I cast my eyes in upward glance
to stare divinity in its face
to see the aura in its place
to catch a glimpse of His sacred plan.

I saw a flash of amazing light
and thunder roared her mighty cry
as forgiveness filled an endless sky
with angels passing by in flight.

Oh how joyous a beauty to behold
saints from ages and ages gone
a reunion of those who had passed on
and the Father with Son and Holy One.

Then I awoke and felt alone
missing what I had just seen
wanting more of what I'd seen.
I'll have to wait until He comes.

Forgive Me?

You ask me to forgive you
for all the tears you made me cry
for the many sleepless nights
when piece by piece I died.

I gave you all that is in me
my love for you will never end
and each time, you say you're sorry
but each time you cause pain again.

You ask me to forgive you
for the many lies you've told.
I know each one so plainly
the new ones are even old.

I took you at your word,
over and over and then
you smiled at me, lovingly
and lied to me again.

You ask me to forgive you
because you think you're lost
you've done some things, some horrible things
and you're frightened of the cost.

My arms are always open
I light for you the path,
you ask me to forgive you,
you should know I already have.

The Fight

I fight this weakness, every day
for it claims victory over me;
the heart, it beats of desire,
with a longing to be free.

I start out straight but falter.
I fight but I don't last long.
I see the prize ahead of me
but this weakness, it is strong.

I know how this conflict ends
it's made plain through His word.
I'll continue the fight, keep the faith
and rely on His guiding word.

No matter the power of this ol' world
and the strength of the fallen one;
I know I'll gain the victory
through the love of the only Son.

Save Me

I came to you, a broken mass
crumbled and torn and hurt.
I ask of you, your masterful hand
that will restore what's lost to whole.

I look to you, for you are love
the greatest of gifts you give
with hands that show your sacrifice
you gave what no other could give.

Please take me and make me your own.
Place your seal in my heart.
Forgive me first for what I have done
I've longed for a transformed heart.

And give to me, the victory
over these things in between us
and let me rest, in perfect sleep
until you come back, to receive us.

and light the path
to your righteousness
for those who
seek you still.

A Mustard Seed

The faith of
a mustard seed,
does not seem
a lot.

We often measure
the wealth we have
in terms of
haves and have not's.

Who would boast
of such a thing
as little as
a simple seed?

And who would dare
to believe
that God
would love even me?

Faith of
a mustard seed

could be
the very thing,

that takes you
from this world of sin
and delivers you
to the King.

Steps to Christ

I always know
that He's with me
even if I cannot see Him.

I hear His voice
inside my head
since my ears they cannot hear Him.

I talk with Him,
I confide in Him,
I ask for his direction.

He answers me
and comforts me,
he shows me His perfection.

His name is love,
His choice... to forgive,
His hands outstretched to us.

His life's work?
…To save our souls
and shower us with His love.

And all He asks
for us to do,
since He formed man from the earth,

is to come to Him
and show love to Him
like He showed us love first.

The Guiding Light

I've stood here at this cross road
wondering which way to go,
the left path is well defined
to the right lies under growth.

I'm not too sure what's up ahead
but it's more than what is here.
I have to make my choice real soon
or else I'll die right here.

Should I follow those, in front of me
and go by what leads them
or take a chance and choose the other
despite what inspires them?

Deep inside I think I know
which of the two to choose,
this could be my last chance
to choose ill would be to lose.

I feel compelled to take the less
traveled path to the right
and place my faith in the Shepherds' hand
as He leads me towards the light.

Follow Me

If you're lost
then follow me,
I'll show you things
you've never seen.
I'll give to you
your every need
and prepare you to
live with me.
I'll change your heart
and give you peace.
I'll quench your thirst
I'll let you see,
the wondrous things
I have in store,
that pain you own
you'll know no more.
I have with me

my father's keys.
The keys to life,
to eternity.
I offer to you
all these things
if you will choose
to follow me.

It's Another Day

Every day is another day
to serve the King of love
to thank Him for his righteousness
and His everlasting love.

We can serve in many ways
no way is too small
showing love to those we know
and to those we don't know at all.

Spend some time in His word
know Him like He knows us.
Feed your relationship with Him
build your faith on trust.

Know that He is in control
when this world feels off tilt.
And call His name to rebuke sin
and aim to do His will.

Start each day with His name
greet Him as you would a friend.
Let the world see Him in you,
let the new day begin.

Keep Me in the Dark

Please leave the lights turned off,
for I have become accustomed to the dark.
Long since I've seen the light of the truth.
I'm ok with living in the wrong.
Please don't turn the light of truth on me.
Please don't show me what I need to see,
for if you show me what I should do,
then the responsibility is left to me.
Please let me stay in the dark.
I'm alright with what I can't see,
although the light will show me the truth,
the darkness has become comfortable to me.
What would I do if you gave me the truth?
What would I do if the darkness was through,
if you turned on the light that showed the truth?
Then I would be accountable too.
So keep me in darkness,
I'll be fine. I'll make it like I always do.
I'll take my chance and stumble on.
I'll feel and fumble my way through.

Keep Me in the Dark is a sad commentary about where many of us are
in our lives. Many of us would rather live a comfortable lie than to live
the truth. We submerge ourselves in familiar things, things that we may

know to be un-Godly but have become our way of life. I doubt many of us would come right out and say the words to the poem, but by our actions, many of us live those words. I believe it's better to be right in the truth than to be comfortable in a lie.

An Answered Prayer

I have prayed, for forty years,
I've been married for forty one.
Waiting patiently to hear the voice,
of the Comforter, of The Chosen One.
I rely, on the strength,
that He has allowed for me.
I give Him praise, I give Him thanks,
for things I have yet to see.
I know He hears me. I know He sees,
the struggles that I've gone through,
but I hold fast to His promise to me,
that He will bring me through.
A miracle from Him has come to me,
for the answer, to my prayer.
I see my husband fast asleep
with the bible also there.
In forty years, never once
have I seen my husband read.
In forty years I have tried,
to show him, God in me.
And now, this night
I've lived to see
the answer to my prayer.
The man I love, with the book I love,
sitting in his favorite chair.

A Sinners Prayer

I approach the thrown of God
on bended knee,
to give thanks for my blessings.

The Holy Spirit brings to me
the remembrance of
life's sacred lessons.

The seed sown through the ages
and the harvest there of
the saints we read about,

Adam, Noah, Abraham, John,
Matthew, Mark, Luke, and Moses,
and how he led the people out.

The remembrance of these
Holy men of God
encourages me in my daily life,

and gives me an example
of the love of God,
and the merciful gift of His Son the Christ.

I pray for strength.
I pray for direction.
I pray for miracles to come.

I give thanks to Him.
I give praise to Him.
I give Him my heart, my love.

I thank you God
for your precious Son
the love of Jesus given to me.

I surrender my heart
and all I own
to be used to draw others to thee.

Do You Know Him?

Whom is it who does these things,
commands both the winds and water,
raised again, those who were dead?
Ask that question of Jairus' daughter.

Whom is it who can heal the sick
of such a lifelong disease
give sight to a helpless blind man
and allow the mute to speak?

This royal one was born,
without great notice to Him
from the very one's
who should have noticed Him.

Yet He lived and died
so they also could live
No one else but Him could bring
the gift of salvation He came to give.

Get to know Him
while yet you still can.
Grow close to Him; love Him;
be a part of His salvation plan.

Yes, He Would

Could you love your brother
or a stranger if you knew
that all the time he smiled
he was plotting to betray you?

Could you lay down your life
for that self-same one
if you knew that in the end
he was the disloyal one?

How would it be
to partake of bread
with the one you knew
would sell your head?

And how would you feel
to know in your heart
that there were those
who doubted from the start?

And to give up a thrown
even for a time
to become a lesser one
even for a time.

Jesus did and I am glad
no one but Him could have come
the God of love gave to us
the gift of His only Son.

Love Him; accept Him;
allow Him to change your life.
Come to Him; stay with Him
and watch Him change your life.

If His death would have saved
but only a single one
nothing would have changed
the Son still would have come.

Heaven's Bread

If you are hungry
and you seek bread to eat
I say to you now
come, take, eat of me.

I have fed
many others before you
some were nearly starved
some just like you.

Feed from me,
your daily bread
I give life eternal
I am heaven's bread.

Back to Eden

The most beautiful place
there was,
at least to the mortal world.

Perfect in every regard
no pain, no rain,
no death.

Flowers of every kind
bright colors, sweet smells,
undefiled.

A land created
for perfect man
ask Adam, why they left.

There, will come a time
long awaited
by fallen man

when Eden in all
her splendor and glory
will be more perfect than before.

Adam will see
the things he named
a sweet reunion for them.

More perfect than perfect
with one great change,
sin will be there, no more.

Like Noah

Creatures both great and small
two by two
and some five more,

led by the voice of God
a change to come
a storm, a great flood.

All had a chance to come,
for years and years,
he urged… he begged.

But in the end
when the flood did come
there were only eight people saved.

God did what
he had to do
to rid that time of sin.

He promised to them
that obeyed Him,
He would never do that again.

A rainbow He set
to remind us
of the fall,

only eight were saved
none else
answered the call.

We should be
like Noah was,
ready to spend our lives

following God's instruction
to us
letting Him lead or lives.

so build that character
that signifies
that Christ lives in your soul

and lead to Him all you can
like the Godly men
of old.

God's Mouth Piece

God, give to me
the words to say
to speak your truth
in your guided way.

May the spirit
you send to me
express your intent
so others will see,

see your passion
and your love towards us
feel your desire
to be with us.

Let the ears of your flock
hear in me
the message for them
you entrust to me.

Use my voice
to reach your souls
see my desire
as your men of old.

Come I pray
give blessings to me
please use me God
as your mouth piece.

Choose Wisely

In the beginning
when God made man
and placed him in the garden,

He knew that evil was there too
and He went to great lengths
to warn him.

Now eat as you will
freely of these
but of that, don't eat or touch it

for if you fall
and eat of that
you surely will die from it.

But man did eat the forbidden fruit
how could he be lead
to do it?

It was the power
of the tempting one
that talked her first into it.

When we stray from God
we get closer to
the one that's known for evil

for our only choice
is one or the other
if not for God, then for the devil.

Choose ye this day
which one you'll serve
the Creator or the created one.

I'll give you a clue,
if you don't know,
choose the one with the Son.

I Am Saved

The path you've laid
for me to know
the way in which
you desire me to go,

the mercy shown
to me each day
the words the spirit
comes to say,

in spite of me
and all I do
you sent your Son
to save me too.

I praise your name
and worship you,
give thanks and notice
for all you do.

Thank you God,
for loving me.
Thank you God
for saving me.

His Last message to Me

Oh my Lord, what doest thou
to bow down to me to wash my feet?

The King of Kings of sinful man
and you humble yourself to me?

Henry Sanders

Who Am I that you would serve
a mere mortal, a sinful, wretched soul?

I feel ashamed for sitting here;
instead, I should be washing yours.

The one who has a legion on call
waiting for your glorious command,

say your will and it be done
an army to destroy sinful man.

Here you sit before you die
anywhere else you could be

but you are here, at my feet
what message is meant for me?

I must learn, to humble myself,
to put away my selfish pride.

And do for others as you have done
and teach them why you died.

You died for us because of love
the compassion you show to all

and left behind an example of
how to treat and love them all.

Jesus, My New Priority

I come to you because there is no other,
what a wretched statement for me to make.
I've put off what I should have done;
I pray that it's not too late.
I come to you a broken shell,
a man in search of a home.
I give to you my heart, my will,
my praise to you alone.
Accept my gift that I bring to you,
use me, as your will would be.
Take my soul into your own
I beg you assign space for me.
I should have placed you first in my life,
forgive my lack of priority.
From this point on come what will be
I will make of you now,
my first priority.

My Trip Home

I have been given
a precious gift
I know when I
will die.

I see the end
approaching me
as my time here
draweth neigh.

I won't leave
with pomp and fair
no spectacle for you
to behold.

I'll slip away
most silently
many won't know
I'm gone.

But those who knew
of me the most
will know
I loved the Lord.

I lived my life
as he did his
us two
on one accord.

I hope to see
the one's I've touched
as I introduced them
to my King.

And as I lay
in peaceful state
my breath
given back to Him.

Oh death where is
thy victory?
For in time
I'll rise and then

meet the saints
above the ground
as we rush
to unite with our King.

But for now I'll keep
my spirits up
and lift up Christ
to all,

give Him the praise,
and thanks
and glory,
the Lamb deserves it all.

Don't cry for me
a sadden tear
I've waited for this
too long.

This is the next step
in my journey here
the trip that
takes me home.

Finally

Don't cry for me
why would you
anyway?

It sounds as if you're in the dark
it sounds like you don't
know the way.

This time I spent, with you,
is smaller than a droplet,
in the sea,

but where I go
when I awake
is measured in eternity.

So, please don't shed,
a tear for me,
save them for another day.

I'm about to start
my sleep,
I'm finally on my way.

Get Ready

Candles a top
a birthday cake
show proof
of my time here.

Another year
has come and gone
some friends
passed on this year.

Each time I hear
about a loss
I can't help but wonder
about their soul,

and how they spent
the time they had
and were they
ready to go.

Life is such
a precious gift
each moment
a miracle from Him,

a time to devote
our lives to Thee
and to lead other souls
to Him.

So spend your time
to prepare your heart
and rid your
life of sin.

So you'll be ready
when deaths angel calls
to meet Christ,
when He comes back again.

What Did You Do Today?

Before I go to bed at night
I reflect on how the day has been

what things I did or didn't do
and would I do them again.

I ask myself did I speak kind words
did I gossip or tell a lie,

and did I do a full days worth
or did just enough to get by?

Did I shine the light given to me?
Did I lead anyone to Christ?

Not so much by what I said
but more how I lived my life.

Did I make someone feel at ease,
by showing patience and interest in them?

Or did I act better than those around me?
And separate myself from them.

How did others see me today?
Was it today as it always is?

Or did I keep them guessing?
Confused by my unstable whims.

How many times did I say hello,
thank you, please, or smiled?

Did I say God loves you today?
Hum, I haven't done that in a while.

The point of this is to be aware
to think and remember every day,

and to use the time we've been given
to show others around us, the way.

Henry Sanders

Be Transformed

Caterpillars turn into
stunning butterflies,

ugly ducklings into
beautiful swans.

God can transform
a wretched sinner like us

into a champion
to battle His cause.

A piece of clay
formed into man,

spoken, and the sun
and the moon appeared.

Gave His Son
to die for us

with His robe
He dries our tears.

And all He asks
in return

is to give our hearts
to Him

so He can give
to each of us

eternity and
peace with Him.

Perfect Peace

Imagine if you will
just for a moment
is all I ask

a place of perfect peace
where all who's there
are on one accord.

No conflict or strife
the air is clear
fresh and sweet

and all who's there
in perfect peace
really want to be;

a place where sickness
has been healed,
all cares and wants within reach,

one day I pray
that I will be
in that place of perfect peace.

Your Vision

If I could see the world
through your eyes
what would I see?

Would I see the good in others
would I have trouble
seeing what you see?

Would I see the need to forgive
the very same ones
who caused pain for me?

If I had your eyes,
your vision,
your perspective, your view,

would I make the same choices
would I behave the same way,
would I be like you?

Would I be able to see
a soul crying out for rescue
and if I could see like you,

how far would I go
to save that lost soul
what lengths would I go to?

I want to see, what you see
to live like you lived.
I want to be closer to you;

please give me the sight
so that I may see
the world with the vision of you.

My New Best Friend

All my life I've been alone
no one really close to me.

Now, I knew people, don't misunderstand;
but none ever really knew me.

We would talk but superficially
about things that didn't mean much,

the weather, the job, politics some;
cars and toys and such.

I never had that closeness
not until I met you.

To think that you were always here
and I'm just now knowing you.

I have to say, you've change my life
in ways I never thought one could.

And this book you inspired and gave to me
wow! I can't put it down, it's better than good.

You did all this just for me?
I've asked myself why a thousand times.

I'm now learning what closeness means.
Your meaning is much better than mine.

Thank you for doing all these things for me,
for being to me, more than a friend.

And just as you told me in Hebrews 13:5
I'll be here for *you* till the end.

Well Done

Oh my friend,
my weathered friend,
you have served
me faithfully,

done the things
that I have asked
and managed to see,
at least most of me.

We've traveled a ways
the two of us
from wilderness to city
to desert sands

and along the way
I've proven to you
that through faith in me
you can.

No king could stop you
although has tried,
you spoke the words
I gave to thee

and lead a nation
of chosen ones
through a mighty
parted sea.

I show to you
the promised land
you've worked so hard
to see

but you cannot
dwell there in,
but instead you'll dwell
here with me.

I am so amazed by the relationship Moses had with God.

Don't Get Caught in the Rain

I will cause
the sky to cry
and cover the earth
with her tears

for man has gotten
progressively worse
as he's lived these
few short years.

It pains my heart
that I have seen
such evil in those
of me

from the start
those first two
were perfect
just as me

but they did fall
of their own will
the start of
what you see here.

If I did nothing
to stop man's fall
evil would not
stop here.

I'll give to those
all who will
protection and life
for an eternity

but for those
who don't choose Me
my wrath will be great,
they'll see.

Now preach to them,
tell all of them,
what they must do
to be saved,

for the chance I give them
to change their ways
won't be offered
always.

Satan's History

There is a war
in this cosmic place
that started in
another time.

The pretty one
wanted his space
and thought to be
the most divine.

He started with
a whisper soft
and quickly spread
his deceit and lies.

His aim was clear
at whatever cost
to tarnish the King
he must blind their eyes.

How could he succeed
you may ask
and deceive a part
of the perfect host?

He is the master
of his craft
with trickery and cunning
he knew the most.

But in the end
he was expelled
and along with him
a third did fall.

His end will be
in fiery Hell
and the sins he caused
he will bare them all.

Henry Sanders

Until I Go Home

I come to you
because I'm lost
and I'm desperate
to find my way.

It's frightful out here
all alone in the dark
I fear I'll never
find my way.

Shine your glory
so that I may see.
Light the path
beneath my feet.

Forgive me Father
for I have sinned
please dear Lord
accept my plea.

I will go
to any place.
I will leave
on any day.

I will do
as you instruct.
I will say
what you tell me to say.

I am determined, to follow you
and follow you all the way
even though it may not be easy
I have vowed not to quit.

I've read the things that you went through
and all that you gave up
how hard it must have been for you
but your vow was not to quit.

Accept me now,
as I am.
Bless me
to conform,

and allow of me
to forever serve thee
until you
call me home.

Henry Sanders

I Want to Go Home

I have seen
throughout my life
a tendency to
repeat,

the very things
that I should not
it's the Israelite
in me.

I've been taught
right from wrong
you've made your
statues known

but along the way
I get out of step
and I end up
far from home.

Home is you
this I believe
and I remember
the joy within

my intentions are good
my desire is strong
but I stumble
and fall… again.

I pick myself up
as best as I can
reach out to you
for your steady reach

I long for victory
over that which entangles me
for you
are the home I seek.

Sinners Anonymous

Hi. I'm Tom.
Hello, Tom.
Glad to be here.
It has been three hours,
fifteen minutes
since I've last sinned.
I feel the pressure
to give up and sin again
but I'm determined
to stay strong
and stay clean.
I ask for your prayers,
your support,
your strength,
as I continue
my sobriety from
sin.

Henry Sanders

Adam's Story

I read today
about Adam
and how perfect
in His image
he was made;
the plan of the Creator
for Adam's life
and the relationship
they both shared.
Adam, the first earthling
the father of us all
allowed sin
to lead him away.
He lost his position in Eden
and his life now
would forever be changed.
Learn from the error
of Adam
don't lose out on
what God has for you.

Show Me Truths

God, I am but
a simple one
no great things
have I done.

Without keen intellect
I get confused;
but I know
I do love you.

I ask of you
to impart to me
the sense to understand
these words from Thee.

An interpretation,
spirit led,
to lead my way,
may I be fed?

Show me truths
I beg of you,
make known to me
what I must do.

Give me clear
the sight I need
save my soul
this is my plea.

Henry Sanders

What Will Your Book Reveal?

When they read your book
the book of your life
what will your book reveal?

Your heart felt thoughts
secrets too
all, will be, unconcealed.

Deeds, both good
and bad
will be made visible, to see.

The thoughts you hold
known only to you
these also will be seen.

Will you be proud,
will you be ashamed,
when God reads your life story?

Start today,
this very day,
to live your life to God's glory.

While You Still Can

Carefree days
and careless ways
not much thought
about future things.

Self-indulgences
negative influences
tomorrow will come
who cares what it brings.

I live for the moment
snub atonement
when my time comes
I'll go…right?

I have no control
over where I'll go
I've got other things
to keep me up at night.

But I won't stop you.
Pray if you want to.
Don't concern yourself over me,
I'll be just fine.

You won't be the first
and I'm far from the worse.
People have been preaching
since the beginning of time.

Henry Sanders

When I see the end
I'll get right then
meanwhile, I've got
places to go.

I'll talk with you next week.
I'll be just fine, you'll see.
Maybe we can read a little,
study the bible…you know.

Yes, officer, that's him.
What happened to him?
I just talked with him
last week.

(the officer)
He drank too much,
flipped his truck.
He was pronounced
dead at the scene.

He never saw his end coming;
never once, stopped running.
What he didn't do
he'll never get done.

Learn from this tragic story.
Live life to God's glory.
Get right with God
before your end comes.

Revelation 19

Oh how glorious a sight
to behold.
Nothing has prepared me
for this.
Ten thousand times
the magnitude,
a once in a lifetime event.
The trumpet yells
a deafening sound
all look toward the
approaching King
and as told,
the wicked meet the ground
and those who've died
meet their King.
And when that ceremony
concludes in grand fair
we left standing
ascend in the air,
to meet our King.

Henry Sanders

You Reap What You Sow

The way I've done things
has not always been
in the best interest of
those around me.

I've said harsh things
made many snap decisions
did not always consider
those around me.

I've professed to be,
a son of the King
often quick to remind
those around me.

I've corrected many
wayward souls
all for the benefit of
those around me.

Now as I lay
on the eve of my last day
I'm really not surprise,
there's no one around me.

The best way to have friends is to be a friend.

As I Lie Dying

As I lie alone in fear
being pushed to within
inches of my life,

being left for dead
by those who
would gladly do me harm,

I lie dying.

I opened my mouth
but could not speak
not a sound would summons rescue.

In a state of shock,
life leaving me,
I close my eyes, while,

I lie dying.

Through half closed eyes,
I see a light,
and a hand reaches out to me.

In an instant I feel
sure relief,
as my breath comes back to me.

I'm not dying.

Henry Sanders

I feel strong hands
lift me up,
in a way I cannot describe.

He places me
near to the street
in the path of passersby,

as I'm reviving.

I wake up here,
with you standing there,
clenched hands, praying for me,

I met my Angel
in an alley last night
he came to me,

as I lie dying.

There have been many accounts where someone in trouble or despair
was rescued by an unknown being. Often times never having seen the
rescuer before or again after the event. I do believe we have guardian
angles around us, protecting us. And at any given time, rescuing us.

Under Construction

I'm asking for a make over
a renovation, a redo.

I want to be less of me.
I want to be more of you.

Replace this defective heart
with one that beats for you.

Remove this doubt that binds me.
Give me faith like Abraham.

Help me change my sinful self.
I don't like the man I am.

Rewrite my blueprint, my design.
Let the Holy Spirit move in me.

I want a structure in which you'll dwell.
I want a house where you will be.

This is not to suggest, in any way, that God designed flaws in us, but we, unlike Adam and Eve, were born into sin. The aim here is to be made right by the Holy Spirit.

Reclaim Me

I can't do this by myself,
I know that now.
I've done pretty much everything
that I know how.
This struggle just gets harder
and I fear I'm losing ground.
I need an intervention,
of the divine kind.
Father, I call out to you
to catch me from my fall.
Place surety under my feet.
Save me, I pray,
rescue me from me.
Give to me, my own mustard seed.
Put me back on the right path,
and strengthen me in my walk,
not to sound impatient,
but I refuse to be lost.
I give myself back to you,
reclaim me please, won't you?

The Master of Deceit

Oh serpent, most unusual,
thou can speak.
What message have you
to give to me?

Oh most beautiful lady,
you noticed thee,
it flatters me greatly
that you find interest in me.

I'll tell you the things
that you want to hear,
don't be ye afraid,
come nearer my dear.

This tree in which
I am in
is not what
you think it to be,

for I have spent
much time up here
and nothing painful
has happened to me.

Its yield is most plentiful
and tasty too;
no other like it
but I'm sure you know.

Take, and eat,
don't worry, it's good.
God said don't,
but He won't know.

That's a girl, take a bite.
Soon your eyes
will know the truth.
You will be as smart as He.

Now find that man
that He giveth thee,
share with him

so his eyes will also see·

I have to go now
but I'll be around·
I'm proud of you
for what you've done·

The key to life
is no mystery,
trust me on this,
we're gonna have some fun·

Although I doubt any of us have had a conversation with a serpent, we probably have faced things that were and are still, enticing to us. It may seem that the enticing thing is talking to us; telling us to engage in behavior we know to be wrong. Just like little babies, we are often drawn to flashy things. And just like babies, many of us can't seem to resist.

Don't Look Back

Come quickly we must flee,
away from this place
that was our home.

Things have gotten out of control,
it is not safe,
even in our home.

The streets are filled
with much wickedness,
every evil of every heart.

No more love for humanity,
greed and lust and selfishness,
have taken over every heart.

This place is cursed.
This place will fall.
This place will cease to be.

Every inhabitant who will stay
for love of this, what has become,
will also cease to be,

so, quickly come,
let's flee this place.
We must leave the home we've known.

We must trust
in the God of Abraham,
the one who rules from the thrown.

Don't look back
upon thy doom,
straight ahead we must walk.

But her heart was heavy
to leave her home
and there becomes a pillar of salt.

God Owns Time

I know those, who pray to God
and place onto Him a time
in which He has, to respond
before they start to whine;

kneel down to pray with pleading words
to recite a familiar chant,
then watch the clock with folded arms
before they start their rant.

They resolve that God is late.
They need intervention now,
if it doesn't come, when they say
they rush their spirits down.

Then Satan whispers to them.
He does what he's best at doing,
causes them an independent act,
that pulls them closer to him.

When they become ensnared and trapped
their vision becomes obscured.
The truth is harder to discern,
when you like what you are doing.

But God stills tries to reach them
and pull them back to His ways.
Have mercy on their wayward souls,
before the end of days.

Be patient my dear loved ones
as patient as our brother Job,
for God has no limit of time,
at least that anyone knows.

Death is the Start

Hear me Lord, I do pray,
we're not prepared for you to leave.
We need you here to guide our way.
Show your strength, say you'll stay,
bound our captors so they'll believe.

Call your angels, that multitude,
the number of which no man knows.
You said no man could do to you
what your Father didn't allow them to.
Expose your glory so they may know.

If you are who you claim to be
then why go through this senseless plan?
Show yourself so we may see
take the thrown in front of thee
prove that you're no mortal man.

I can't stay, past time with you.
I am here to fulfill what has been
told.
This thing I have, I alone must do,
I do this thing because of you.
And when it's done I must go.

Don't hold evil, in your hearts.
Remember the things I've told to you.
I must go; it's time to start,
you must preach; death is my part.
I go now to prepare for you.

Of course this isn't scriptural. This is what I imagined could have been said by Jesus to those who would rather have destroyed his captures and liberated the Israelites. I envision that some of the Israelites didn't understand why he had to die instead of taking his place as King and ruling over the Romans. I imagine some believed that since he was God's Son, all he had to do was say the word and it would have been all over, without any pain and suffering. But of course, that was not the plan of salvation.

Come Whoever Will

Inspiration comes to me
to show me things I need to see
to lead my path to the Christ
to use His life to pattern by.

I see the sun and think of Him.
I see my children, He gave me them.
The wind blows gently across my face
I know His spirit is in this place.

I think of Eden, perfection then,
this was before her tenants sinned
and how broken hearted He became
that life from then, would be changed.

Sin was born, now man must die.
Jesus Himself the sacrifice,
He gave His life so we can live,
come to Him all who will.

The King is Coming Home

The wait is nearly over
my Son is coming home.
The final step in His journey
this thing He must do alone.

He went because He wanted to,
that's just the way He is.
He knew that they would be afraid
that Satan would exploit their fears.

He taught with patience and with love
and He lived the life He described.
I asked if they would follow Him
He replied, "Father I tried."

I told Him that I loved Him
and that He has made me proud
and not to focus too much on
the hatred from Satan's crowd.

Now rest my son, it's over.
You've done all that I've asked you to.
In three short days you'll see me again
and Moses, he's here too.

He'll welcome you at heaven's gate,
as the angels rejoice with song,
it has only been some thirty-three years
but for them, that's been too long.

Rest my Son, my only one.
Your thrown is waiting for you
you've done this thing for fallen man
now let's see what they'll do for you.

Again, this exchange is not found in the Bible. It's a conversation I
imagined in present day that I think could express what happened during
the crucifixion, resurrection, and reunification of Jesus with God the
Father and the heavenly population.

Forgive and Live

My husband heard me praying one night.
I usually have the bedroom door closed.
I guess in my haste to speak with God,
I didn't notice the door wasn't closed.
I started my prayer as I always did.
I thanked Him first, for saving me,
I asked for forgiveness for all my sins
and to bestow more patience to me.
Then like clockwork, since before I can remember when
I said a prayer for my husband.
I asked God to forgive all his sins
and to be to me a better husband,
to treat me like he treats his "special friend."
To show me compassion with some respect,
I prayed to feel he loved me again.
I asked God to touch his heart
so that he may feel happy and then,
to recommit his love to me
after all, he did marry me.
Then I heard the door close,
as I finished my words.
I then feared the worst out of him
to my surprise, he never said a word
but I'm sure in my heart, he heard.
I let it go; I couldn't change what was done.
The very next day he came to me
and he told me that I was the one.
He confessed to me
that he had betrayed me
and he asked if I could ever forgive him.
I said I could, I said I would,

since Jesus had many times forgiven me.
That all happened forty years ago.
We've been closer than ever, since then.
The door is always opened now, every time we pray.
We've grown so much, the two of us,
we're Christians, we're married, we're friends.

Come What May, I'm Saved

The Dr. said he didn't understand
how I sat so calmly after the news.
Most others like me would fall apart
but I did not, because of what I knew.
I know that I am saved,
perhaps not in the physical.
Years ago, my life was transformed,
I was introduced, to the King.

This life, this body, a temporary thing
but there is eternity with Jesus, the King.
I don't fear what's in front of me.
I, instead, pray His will to be.
Come what may, I will keep,
like Job of old, my integrity.
In life or death, I will still be
saved by the grace He gives me.

What's in a Name?

My neighbor said he's a Christian,
this was news to me.
Every time I've waved hello
he seems to stare through me.
He's asked my help, several times,
with chores and simple things
but never after asking him,
has he one time helped me;
why just a few, days ago,
when I was running late,
my car wouldn't start, battery was dead,
I asked him for his help.
He looked at me
with unconcern
said he was off to bed.
I don't know the things I should,
and I'm not where I should be
but I've been around Christians before
and he's not one to me.

The First War Ever

The first war ever waged
may not be what you believe.
The root of it may not be plain.
No bloody soldiers there lay slain.
No other countries to engage,

is that what you believed?
This war that I am speaking of
was like no other since.
No blood was shed.
No massive dead.
The victors' armed with love
have been loving ever since.
Worship was the start of it
and pride very soon set in.
The created one that was next to Him
wanted he, to be equal Them,
was determined not to quit.
And so the war begins.
Treason spread throughout the land
fueled by lies and deceit.
The anti-one had gained support
tried to destroy divinity's court.
They rallied to make their stand.
He wanted that sacred seat.
The Mighty Voice called out to them;
the war would go no more.
A silence fell across the land.
The Ruler and Son raised their hands,
spoke to he that mislead them.
"It is done, now you must go."
A third of them left that day.
What a sad day that was.
The leader of the fallen few
vowed to them he wasn't through,
at that point he could have stayed
but instead he fell to earth.
And here remains the evil one.
He's doing what he does best.

He's better now than days of old,
if you're careless he will steal your soul;
but the Mighty One gave us His Son
that we may pass his test.

This poem was inspired by the accounts of Revelation, chapter 12 and
other books in the bible that talk about Satan being banished out of
heaven and having deceived a third of the angles, who were thrown out
of heaven with him.

Does it Matter the Day?

What's this thing about a certain day?
Does it matter and to whom?
All the days are created ones
why does it matter and to whom?
The word does say to honor a day,
to keep it holly the word does say
but which day, does it say?
Does it even matter anyway?
What if I decide the day I use
to fulfill thus sayeth the word?
A day that also pleases me
what's wrong with that any way?
As long as I give unto a day
to make it holly and set aside
would not that be the thing to do?
I'll pick the day, I'll decide.
What is this, the Sabbath Day?
The day the Lord took a rest;
it was the last one that He made

would not the first one have been the best?
What harm would I cause
if I make the change?
Surely the Lord will understand;
for wasn't this day made for man?
Though the Lord said the Sabbath Day
and though it be the seventh day
I will choose the first of days
and honor it in my own way.
For this is the day our father's kept;
learned men made the change,
it they didn't honor the seventh day,
does it really matter, anyway?

Creation Week

How cool is it
when you think of it
creation took a week.
Some would say
even now today
that we all just evolved.
To seriously think
that in a wink
with a bang life came to be.
But from God's word
and I believe His word
He created you and me.

The Parable Purpose

I speak in parables
not for want of words to say
for I know that which
you can understand.
I come to you
on your own terms
because I love you so
and long for you to understand.
If I were to say to you
that which I know
you would fail to comprehend
as result, you wouldn't grow.
So listen intently as I speak
in these ways you can understand.
Simple in means for you to relate
this, blame on sin, not My plan.

Victory Over Sin

God please give me
the strength I need
to turn from these sins
that still taunt me.
Give me I pray
a different heart
that gives me joy
to do my part

to spread your word
and live the life
to tell the world
why you came and died
but remind them too
that you live again
and in you is our victory
to overcome our sins.

Your Sorrowful Child

Forgive me sweet Jesus,
I apologize,
for breaking your heart
and for making you cry.
I have done some
sinful things,
I must admit
again and yet again.
My intentions at first
are strong and good,
to do that which
I know I should.
But weak am I
in strength of soul
and caught in the grasp
of the anti-one's hold.
I pray to you
for strength of soul
and power of will

and wisdom to know
and to be
your measure of clay
to be formed by you
and shaped in a way
that pleases you
and makes you smile
forgive me father,
your sorrowful child.

New Testament Intro.

My eyes are worn
from crying all night.
I read for the first time
about the death of Christ.
The greatest love story
I have ever read,
to know this was done for me
now I can live instead.
The things He put Himself through,
the pain and torture and all.
He would have died if only for one
but He came and died to save us all.
I shall read more about this Christ.
I feel a need to get closer to Him.
And If He wants me, to live like Him,
then that's what I'll do with my life.

I've Been There all Along

God where were you
as I cried last night
for fear I would die
in the storm?
And where were you
when my mother died
and left me here
in this world all alone?
And what about the time
I prayed to you
when I got attacked
and came close to losing my sight?
And remember when
I lost my job, you know,
the week before
the office caught fire?
And I've asked you over
and over again,
please don't let me
live alone,
all I have
is this mutt of a dog
he won't leave my side
and he eats me out of house and home.
I've asked for wisdom
and guidance and truth
what should I do?
I just don't understand.
And this new pastor at church
he keeps calling me
"See you Wednesday night", he says.

Wow! He's such an annoying man.
Do you even hear me, Lord?
Have you given up on me?
Am I really that evil?
Am I lost?
What's this in the mail?
I wonder who it's from?
All it says is
"He paid the cost".

Arise Anew

When you do wrong
against your God
like many a man will do,
He won't forget or forsake you
to some that may seem odd.
Before life was breathed into you
and your existence recorded above
God had devised a salvation plan
to save His created, fallen man.
This is His meaning of love.
Christ was seated upon His thrown,
in dialogue with His God.
He left His seat to dwell beneath,
to show this world the power of peace,
to give us the message of God.
When in sin we stumble and fall
and in sorrow we lose our way

call on God to wash your heart.
Arise in Him with a clean, fresh start,
for tomorrow is yet, a brand new day.

Reminded by Bad Memories

Not a day goes by
these last few years
that I don't think of things
I've said and done.
The people I've hurt
with selfishness,
the awful things
I once considered fun.
I've been to the edge,
almost fell in,
but now I'm back here
purely by the grace of God.
And I won't leave
this place again,
those bad memories
die hard.

Henry Sanders

The Upper Room

We all sat there and did not move
an awkward quietness filled the room.
Why was not a servant here?
That was my thought as I sat there.
Who will serve the lot of us?
Which of the twelve will be served first?
But no one came to that upper room
to clean our dust or serve us food.
The Master arose and started to speak.
He taught to us, humility.
I felt ashamed as he came to me
and gently began to wash my feet.
The King of Kings, the only Son,
the world's only hope, the chosen one,
had humbled Himself to serve even me
taught us that day, how we should be.
Serve one another, dismiss selfish pride,
soon after that, they killed the Christ.
What I learned in that upper room
I've lived to show to even you.

Judas

Oh my God,
what have I done?
I turned Him in,
the Father's Son.
I did not mean
to cause this thing,
I only wanted
to force the King.
What I did
was for my own cause.
He came to earth to save
all who would be lost.
But I wanted Him
to favor only me
and lift me up
so the others could see
and in my new power
perhaps envy me?
But cursed be to me
for what I've done
I betrayed my King,
the Father's Son.

My idea of what Judas may have thought.

Peter

Ashamed am I
for what I've done
fear for my life,
this wretched one,
led me to do
that which I've done.
I've known Him
but a little while.
I've seen His patience
I've seen Him smile.
I've felt His love
like an innocent child.
He has taught to us
many important things.
He's caused the angles
in heaven to sing.
He's promised to us
no less than everything.
He's about to die
to save yet me,
as I have denied Him
even times three.
He told me so
the truth to be.
I see Him there
at His life's end
perfect from start
with a perfect end.
He still loves me
He's still my friend.
I will commit to thee

my life that remains,
from your ways
I will not refrain.
I'll walk your path
till we meet again.

He Loves Us Still

Jesus my friend, welcome home.
I've watched as the scene saddened me,
after all we did for them, down there
they still refuse to see.
The years I spent leading them
my life's work all for your cause.
They still don't seem to understand
that you're the way for us all.
When I saw them nail you to the cross,
it was as if I felt your pain.
But after resting on the Sabbath day
you rose to life again.
We filled heaven's space with jubilee
high praises and honor to you.
We cheered so loud "He lives, He lives",
we wanted all below to hear it too.
Don't be sad, you did all you could.
Remember what you once said to me?
"Well done my friend, I am pleased",
now we must all wait and see.
The spirit is strong, he knows their will.
You left them in good hands with him.

He will guide as both we have,
while you now intercede for them.

What Have We Done?

What have we done
to the Holy One
who came to save
each one of us?
We mocked Him, scoffed Him,
insulted Him, accused Him,
ignored Him, dismissed Him,
betrayed Him, and slew Him.
He came as us.
He lived with us
and what He taught
was for all of us.
But we allowed
the fallen one
to shake us from
the Father's Son.
Woe be to us
for what we've done
we shed the blood
of the Father's Son.

A Prudent Man

Why walk straight into trouble's path
and suffer the woes sure to come?
Why make it easy for the tempter
to do what he has always done?

If you see trouble in your path
choose a different course to walk,
flee from that which appears wrong
make hast away, run don't walk.

Be quick, be wise, and be clear.
Avoid all evil if you can.
Don't volunteer your soul to him
live your life as a prudent man.

A Miracle in My Neighborhood

I know this young man,
I've watched him grow up,
his life very rocky from the start.
His parents tried hard
but no match for their truth,
they knew light; but instead chose the dark.

The ways of the world
were not kind to them.
Their young son took the brunt of their pain.
He learned the hard way
though the sun may shine
his life, would constantly see rain.

At times through his life
he couldn't understand why,
no rhyme to the reason of his life.
No chance to survive;
the existence he would know
the only way out, was to die.

It's now been, some thirty two years,
here, in this same neighborhood,
life has treated him so hard.
But the miracle I see
now standing before me
is a man who finally found God.

A Hurtful Tongue

We all have
a tongue,
they're pretty much
all alike.

They determine
our taste of things

and tell us
what we like.

Bitter or sweet
spicy or mild
tart or sour
and tastes we identify,

but our tongues
can do another thing—
say words
that can ruin lives.

Be careful how
you use your tongue
be aware of what
you say.

Words thrown out
without regard
could cause pain
that won't go away.

Called to Speak

Are you strong enough to stand for God
to share His message with His fold,
to tell them the stories told of old,
to preach to them so they will know,
the joy of serving their God?

This message may not be eagerly received,
for some may be called and refuse to go.
Some may move but move too slow.
God calls some to let us know,
His salvation plan for us all.

If you are called, will you go,
to spread the gospel in all the land,
to tell the story of the Son of man,
to explain the scars in His hands,
and how He died for us?

Come Home

I say
these things to you
because of love I do,
to lead you, guide you, as you go.
Surely I desire you to know your way.
Learn to listen to what I say.
Come home, come home, come home.
I bid you stay,
with me.

Dying to Save Us

What have we done?
May God have mercy on our souls?
He tried to tell us
and we would not hear.
He tried to teach us
and we would not let Him teach.
He said He will return for us.
Let's not ignore Him again.

Even For Only One

I say to you, this day
that you will be with me.
Your heart has been found wanting
and for that I'll set you free.

Now you must forgive your transgressors
as I have shown you how
and pray they be forgiven
that I will save their lives.

Close your eyes and go to sleep.
Rest your weary soul.
I have plans I can't explain
but in time you'll come to know.

I accept your life, you've given me
as we hang here before them all.
Many times I've called out to you
and today you answered my call.

I created you, from the start.
You are a part of me.
And now that you have accepted me
I can go in peace.

I Know Him Not

He who was sent from God
born of one of us
to save humanity--
I know Him not.

He who lived a sinless life
and was never compelled
by selfish pride--
I know Him not.

Though I have seen
miracles He performed
and how He healed the sick
many times before,

even though I'm here tonight
and I fear for what
will become of Him
the man, the Son, the Christ,

the one whom I do know
loves us all the same
and who I know knows me.
I know Him not.

Forgive me my Lord.
I'm sorry.
Three times I denied.

In my mind, what Peter may have said after denying Jesus three times.
Peter had seen many things that Jesus did and said but perhaps of fear of
his own life, still denied knowing Him.

Jesus(Acrostic)

Join the flock that follows Him,

each their own connection with Him.

Say His name and ask Him in.

Unite with His power and His grace.

Stand firm in Him and be saved.

Let Him Amaze You Too

It happened just as they said it would.
The more I get, the more I want.
Things are better understood
when He is in your heart.
He knocks at the door
let Him come in.
You will be
amazed
too.

My End Time

They tell me I don't have much time.
For me, things are quickly running out.

I've had time to re-look things in my life
and I'm making some changes because of it.

I need years to undo the things I've done.
But years, I do not have and that is my great regret.

I have rearranged the list of things I must do
priorities have been shifted and reassigned.

I have moved *you* to the top where you should have been
and I'm sorry I did not see my error before

for what little time I have left
I will spend that time making things right with you.

Many of us will wait until we get a wakeup call from life to realize we have failed to do things we should have been doing all along. The good news is, there's still time to get right with others and especially, with God.

Our Savior

Jesus came to save this wretched world
to trade His life for fallen man
to give him a chance to live
oh what love He shows
oh the love He gives.
No one but Him
could do this
to save
us.

Henry Sanders

Replace My Weakness

Forgive me for my weakness.
If only I had your strength.
I want to please and serve you.
Will you strengthen me?

I consider this to be a very simple, easy, and powerful prayer. I think
many of us have the desire to do right but on our own, lack the power.

Salvation Through You

Sweet words and sounds
that make me smile
I need to smile again.

I remember those days
from years dear and past
and life back then, without pain.

I strayed from you once
but no more, no more
I'm back where I belong.

Forgive me please
I beg of you
and let me enjoy your song.

You make my heart glad
you touch my inner soul
I am inspired by your life.

I know it's through you
that I may achieve
salvation and eternal life.

Your Power In Me

Show me your power,
in my life.
I have the desire
but I am weak.

I have learned
from your life
but I beseech you
to give me power.

Your way is my way.
I want to please you
but sin doeth keep
the pressure on me.

Forgive my weakness
and read my heart
I am your child
but I feel lost.

Give me a new heart
that beats for you
that I may serve you
and only you.

You Are Never Alone

I have prayed as best I can.
I put this issue at your feet.
You know my heart and who I am
and how I fit into your master plan,
please God, rescue me.

Have I suffered long enough?
How much more, must my soul take?
All my life I've had it rough.
I've carried around too much stuff
and I'm praying for a break.

My child I know what you've gone through.
I've known you since before the start
and I've been there standing next to you.
I'm proud of the things I see you do
and you're right, I do know your heart.

I won't allow to come to you,
the things you cannot bear.
And I do have bigger plans for you
and you should know, I won't leave you
no matter what comes, I'll be there.

Your Loving Ways

When you came to me
I was at the lowest point.
I had been there quite some time.

The things that have always been
important to me, didn't seem to be
as important to me as they had been.

My view of my world was distorted and
trouble seemed my only true friend,
what an awful way to exist.

It's funny how what I needed most
had been within my reach all along
I just didn't know it till now.

Thank you for your saving grace
that keeps me in a higher place
as I grow to learn your loving ways.

To Be Saved

Jesus told many what it took
in order for them to be saved.
There were those who heeded His words
but some remain lost, even today.

Keep His commandments
and love one another,
forgive your enemies
as you forgive your brothers,

do unto to those
as you want those to do,
show mercy of heart to them
like God shows mercy to you,

and when a man is down
show him the way up
when a child is poor
help fill his empty cup,

honor those who bore long with you
respect for them will lengthen your days
and do your best to please your God
by changing your sinful ways,

ask for forgiveness
for the wrongs you have done
and pattern your life
after the redeeming one,

give your heart and soul
and will to Him
and He will keep you
always--with Him.

You Live Through Him(Cinquain)

Repent
I say to you
or you will surely die.
But by the blood of Jesus Christ
you live.

INDEX

INDEX

INDEX

INDEX

Henry Sanders